Aunt Mil's
DELICIOUS 100 YEAR OLD
Italian Recipes

JOE BAGNATO
& GEORGE GIULIANI PH. D.

LifeRich Publishing is a registered trademark of The Reader's Digest Association, Inc.

LifeRich Publishing books may be ordered through booksellers or by contacting:

LifeRich Publishing
1663 Liberty Drive
Bloomington, IN 47403
www.liferichpublishing.com
1 (888) 238-8637

Because of the dynamic nature of the Internet, any web addresses or links contained in this book may have changed since publication and may no longer be valid. The views expressed in this work are solely those of the author and do not necessarily reflect the views of the publisher, and the publisher hereby disclaims any responsibility for them.

Any people depicted in stock imagery provided by Thinkstock are models, and such images are being used for illustrative purposes only.
Certain stock imagery © Thinkstock.

ISBN: 978-1-4897-0684-3 (sc)
ISBN: 978-1-4897-0682-9 (hc)
ISBN: 978-1-4897-0683-6 (e)

Library of Congress Control Number: 2016903800

Print information available on the last page.

LifeRich Publishing rev. date: 5/25/2016

To Aunt Mil, who had the foresight to document these recipes on index cards, and also to a little province of Salerno called Sala Consilina, where it all began more than a hundred years ago.

Contents

Preface

Aunt Mil passed away on July 18, 2013, at the age of ninety-six. She got these recipes, now more than one hundred years ago, from her mother, our grandmother, Maria Castrataro, who was born in 1879 in Sala Consilina, a small town in Salerno, where Maria married George Castrataro, our grandfather. They came to America with six children and then had four more children. Aunt Mil was the youngest child, and she eventually became the scholar of the family. She graduated from Brooklyn College with a bachelor's degree and from NYU with a master's degree in French.

On December 25, 2010, at the age of ninety-two, Aunt Mil gave Joe's wife, Dottie, a wonderful Christmas present in a beautiful box with a crocheted cover. She gave Dottie each of her recipes, handwritten on index cards, so they could be carried down to future generations. Upon Aunt Mil's death, Dottie gave those same recipes to members of the family in Aunt Mil's honor. Within two weeks, one of our cousins put together a six-course dinner using mostly Aunt Mil's recipes.

In 1944, Aunt Mil married Anthony Bagnato, who was called by his nickname, Uncle Tuck. All the dinners she cooked were Italian except on Wednesdays and Saturdays. She did this every week through 2011—for sixty-seven years. That comes to 260 Italian meals a year, and Aunt Mil did this for sixty-seven years, bringing her total Italian meals cooked to more than 17,000. After having eaten many of her meals over the years, can certainly attest to the fact that she was qualified as an expert Italian cook.

For us kids who were raised in such an environment—and there was a slew of us—we can remember waking up on Sunday mornings to the aroma of garlic and onions frying in olive oil. We knew that when we got out of bed, we would find delicious meatballs in the kitchen with a pot of "gravy" (as the pasta sauce was called back then) simmering on the stove. Nothing tasted better than fresh meatballs with fresh, soft italian bread dipped into the pot of hot gravy. (Gravy began to be called sauce starting the early 1960s.)

There's no question that the Italian meal is among the most important aspects of the traditional Italian family. It is obvious that Italians have a love affair with food. This is not only about Italian recipes—it's also about what really great food brings to the dinner table: family, belonging, identity, memories, and tradition.

This book will guide you through fifty-two magnificent Italian recipes, along with many tidbits about Italy that we hope you will find enjoyable. We sincerely feel that by writing this book, these precious recipes will not fade away into oblivion. We hope that after reading these recipes, future generations of young chefs and family cooks will preserve them another hundred years. We are proud and pleased to share these treasured recipes with you, and we know they will enhance your dining pleasure.

As our grandmother often said to us, "Mangiare bene." Eat well!

Pasta

Lasagna

Serves 8

1 POUND GROUND BEEF
1/2 POUND OF SAUSAGE
MEAT SAUCE (SEE RECIPE PAGE 56)
PECORINO ROMANO CHEESE, TO TASTE
3 POUNDS RICOTTA
1 POUND LASAGNA
1 POUND MOZZARELLA, CHOPPED

1. Prepare the chopped meat, and mix it as you would for making meatballs, but do not roll into balls. See recipe for meatball on page 67.
2. Take sausage meat out of casing first.
3. In a frying pan, on medium-high heat, cook meatball mixture and sausage together for 15 minutes. Stir often.
4. Add some meat sauce to frying pan, and cook for about 15 minutes.
5. In a 9 × 13–inch aluminum baking pan or dish, layer the lasagna in the order shown below, and cook for about 45 minutes to 1 hour. You can check how hot it is by sticking a knife or fork in the middle and touching the utensil to see how hot it is.

Layering of Lasagna

1. Lasagna
2. Ricotta
3. Mozzarella
4. Meatball/sausage mixture
5. Meat sauce
6. Repeat layering until desired thicknesss

When cooked let stand for 5 minutes. Cut the lasagna to your desired portion size in a criss-cross pattern.

Lasagna, one of the most celebrated of the Italian foods, has a long history. The term *lasagna* comes from the Greek word *lasagnum*, meaning a dish or bowl. The Romans, who ended up using the same style of dish, also developed a food with the same name. The early Italians changed the name from *lasagnum* to *lasagna*. Over the years, the meaning of the word *lasagna* began to change definitions: it began to mean the delicious pasta meal in the dish itself. In modern cooking terms, it now means layers of thin pasta with meat, cheese, and tomato sauce in between the layers.[1]

Linguini with Clam Sauce

White Clam Sauce

Serves 4

**18–24 LITTLENECK CLAMS, OR 3 (6 1/2 OUNCE)
CANS MINCED OR CHOPPED CLAMS
4–5 TABLESPOONS OF OLIVE OIL
3–4 CLOVES OF GARLIC, CHOPPED
ABOUT 5 SPRIGS OF ITALIAN PARSLEY, CHOPPED
SALT TO TASTE
1 POUND OF LINGUINI**

If Using Fresh Clams

- When using hard-shell clams, make sure they are alive by checking that they are tightly closed. If they are not, discard them.
- Clean the clams by running them under cold water and then scrubbing them with a stiff brush.
- Steam the clams. It is best to use just a bit of liquid; use too much, and you'll boil the meat instead of steaming it.
- Add enough liquid to cover the bottom of a deep pan or a stockpot about 1/4 inch deep.
- Heat on medium-high heat.
- When liquid starts to boil, add shellfish. Cover with a tight-fitting lid, and cook until done.
- When they're cooked, the shells will open wide. Cooking time depends on the size of the shellfish. If some of the clams do not open, discard them.
- When finished, drain the clams in a colander, and then put into a bowl. Use the juice in step 5.

1. In a frying pan, heat olive oil and garlic—but do not burn.
2. Add about 1/4 cup of water, and add parsley. Cook over low heat about 4–5 minutes.
3. Add another 1/2 cup of water on medium heat; bring to boil.
4. Lower heat and add clams and their juices for about another 4–5 minutes. Do not overcook clams.
5. In a large pot, add enough water so the linguini is fully submerged, salt to taste, and bring to a boil. Then add linguini and cook to taste.

When cooked place the linguini on serving plates, add the clams and some of the sauce to each plate.

In Italy, you will rarely find linguini made with red clam sauce; also, serving parmesan cheese on top of this dish is not done. This is only a big seller in Italian American restaurants. If you should visit Italy, expect to have linguini with white clam sauce and no cheese.

Linguini with Mussels

Serves 4

2–3 POUNDS OF MUSSELS
2–3 TABLESPOONS OLIVE OIL
2–3 CLOVES OF CHOPPED GARLIC, OR 1/4–3/8 TEASPOON GARLIC POWDER
1 BUNCH BASIL LEAVES DICED
1 SMALL CAN OF TOMATO PASTE
1 CAN OF TOMATOES, CHOPPED OR DICED
1 POUND LINGUINI OR SPAGHETTI

1. Clean the mussels by running them under cold water. Discard any opened or cracked mussels. In a pot filled with about 1/2 cup of water, put mussels in pot and cover. Steam them until they open.
2. In a pan, heat olive oil and garlic, but do not burn.
3. Add tomatoes, basil, and salt to taste. Cover and cook over medium heat; stir to prevent sticking and burning of tomatoes.
4. After about 15 minutes, add 1 cup of water and 1–2 teaspoons of tomato paste. Stir and cook for about 15–20 minutes. This is to be a light fish sauce, so if it is too thick, add some water.
5. Add the mussels. Stir and shut off heat so that mussels are not overcooked.
6. Boil water, and cook the linguini or spaghetti per the instructions on the box.

Place the linguini in serving plates, add the mussels and sauce as desired.

Avoid serving spaghetti or linguini at formal parties. Short pasta, such as ziti or penne, is much easier to serve.

Manicotti

Serves 8

3 POUNDS RICOTTA
1 POUND MOZZARELLA, CHOPPED
4 CUPS ALL-PURPOSE FLOUR
1 TEASPOON SALT
4 EGGS, SLIGHTLY BEATEN
ABOUT 2/3 CUP WATER
8 CUPS OF MARINARA SAUCE (SEE MARINARA RECIPE ON PAGE ?); YOU MAY USE MORE SAUCE IF DESIRED

1. Mix the ricotta and the chopped mozzarella thoroughly; set aside.
2. Combine flour and salt in a mixing bowl. Add eggs and enough water to make the dough firm.
3. On a lightly floured board or pastry surface, knead dough until firm.
4. Cover dough with a bowl; let it rise and breathe for 15–30 minutes.
5. When dough is ready, divide into quarters.
6. Roll out dough on lightly floured board until very thin.
7. Cut into about 4-inch circles.
8. When finished cutting the circles, place them in boiling water and cook for about 3–5 minutes. Do not overcook the manicotti, because you will be placing them in the oven when stuffed.
9. Take manicotti out of the water so they do not cook any further.
10. Place manicotti on flat surface, adding the cheese filling to one side of the manicotti. Have a small bowl of water to dip your fingers in; then moisten the edge, fold the other side over the filling, and press lightly with a fork to seal it closed.
11. In a 9 × 13–inch baking pan or dish, put marinara sauce on the bottom, and place the manicotti in the dish. When finished, ladle marinara sauce across the top of the manicotti. Cover with aluminum foil, and bake for about 20–25 minutes.

When cooked you can plate immediately

Note: I do not use parsley when I make the filling, but you may use it if you like.

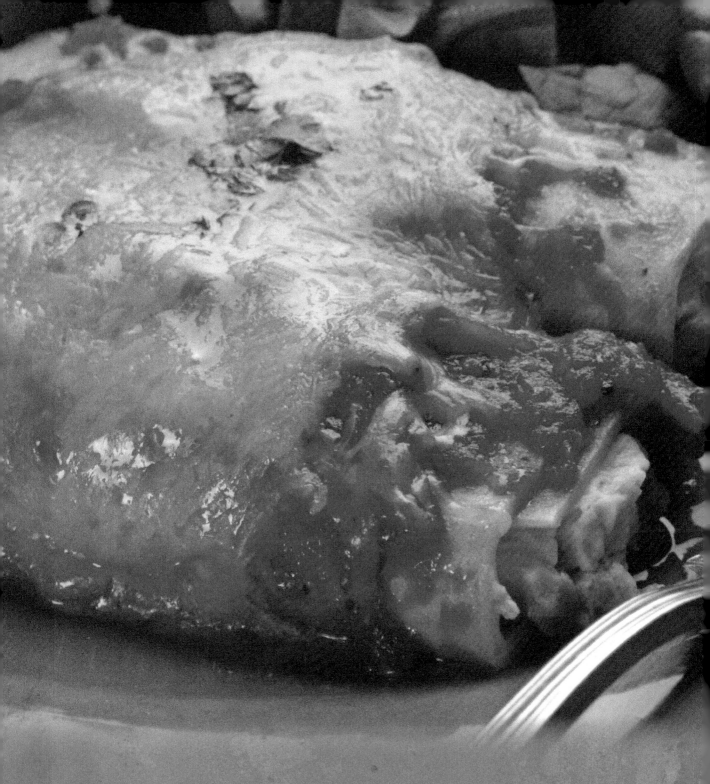

Manicotti means small muffs and was originally made with crepes rolled around a savory ricotta and parmesan cheese filling. In southern Italy, pasta dough for manicotti was used instead of crepes. Aunt Mil is from southern Italy, and so this is the type manicotti we loved and grew up on.

Pasta with Broccoli and Bacon

Serves 4

1 PACKAGE BACON NOT TOO FATTY
2 CLOVES GARLIC, MINCED
1 ONION, FINELY CHOPPED
BUNCH BROCCOLI
1/2 CUP CHICKEN BROTH
2–3 TABLESPOONS PECORINO ROMANO CHEESE
SALT AND PEPPER
1 POUND ROTELLI OR ZITI

1. Cut bacon strips into 3 parts.
2. In a skillet, cook bacon pieces over medium heat until they begin to brown. Pour out some dripping if there is too much.
3. Stir in garlic and onions; cover and cook until onions are soft, about 4–6 minutes.
4. Broccoli should be cut into separate florets (see note below), with the tender parts of the stem cut into chunks.
5. Increase heat to medium high; add the chicken broth and broccoli. Cover and cook until the broccoli is tender yet still green, about 7–8 minutes. Stir in cheese, and season to taste with salt and pepper.
6. You may substitute Cubed beef cut in smaller pieces for step number one. In step 5 instead of ½ cup of chicken brothe add ¾ of a cup.
7. In a large pot, bring to a boil enough water to cover the pasta. Add pasta, stir, and cook according to the box's instructions. When cooked, drain well and toss with the broccoli mixture.

Note: How to floret broccoli.

1. Cut the steam off at the very top to make sure the individual florets fall away as you cut.
2. Take the individual florets and cut them in half. Depending on your taste, you may then cut them in quarters or leave the florets whole.

When cooking garlic, always use medium heat, and stir it often. If the oil becomes too hot, garlic can become bitter.

Ravioli

For Filling

3 POUNDS RICOTTA
1 POUND MOZZARELLA, CHOPPED
2 EGGS
4 SPRIGS PARSLEY, FINELY CHOPPED
PECORINO ROMANO CHEESE, GRATED

For Dough

4 CUPS ALL-PURPOSE FLOUR
ABOUT 2/3 CUP OF WATER
4 EGGS, SLIGHTLY BEATEN
1 TEASPOON SALT

For plating

8 cups marinara sauce (see page 54)

1. Mix the ricotta, chopped mozzarella, 2 eggs, parsley, and pecorino romano cheese thoroughly; set aside.
2. Combine flour and salt in a mixing bowl. Use the 4 slightly beaten eggs and enough water to make the dough firm.
3. On a lightly floured board or pastry surface, knead dough until firm.
4. Cover dough with a bowl; let it rise and breathe for 15–30 minutes.
5. When dough is ready, divide into quarters.
6. Take one quarter at a time. On a lightly floured board, roll out until very thin.
7. Cut into 2- or 3-inch squares, or 3-inch circles.
8. Take a cut square, and place about 1 tablespoon of filling in the center of the square.
9. Cover with the empty square; have a small bowl of water to dip your fingers in. Moisten the edges of the filled square. Press together with a fork around all the edges.
10. Place ravioli in boiling water, and cook for about 5–6 minutes or until they float. You can take a small portion of the edges to see if they're done.
11. It is best to take the ravioli out of the water with a slotted spoon so they don't leak or fall apart.

Ladle the plate with sauce, add the ravioli and cover them with sauce.

In Italy, ravioli was traditionally made at home. The filling varied according to the region in which one lived. In Sala Consilina, the filling of choice was ricotta, parsley, and grated cheese.

Stuffed Shells

Serves 8

3 POUNDS RICOTTA
2 EGGS
1 POUND MOZZARELLA, CHOPPED
3 CUPS FRESH PARSLEY CHOPPED
PECORINO ROMANO CHEESE, GRATED
SALT TO TASTE
1 SIXTEEN OUNCE BOX LARGE SHELLS
1 TEASPOON OLIVE OIL
8 CUPS MARINARA SAUCE (SEE MARINARA SAUCE RECIPE
ON PAGE 54) YOU MAY USE MORE SAUCE IF DESIRED

1. In a bowl, mix eggs, ricotta, mozzarella, parsley, pecorino romano cheese, and salt. Set aside.
2. Put shells in boiling water; add salt to taste and 1 teaspoon of olive oil. Cook for about 15 minutes.
3. Strain and fill each shell with the filling.
4. In a roasting pan, ladle marinara sauce on the bottom of pan, spreading evenly. Place each shell into the pan.
5. When pan is filled with the shells, ladle marinara sauce across the top of shells.
6. Bake for about 20 minutes.

In Italy, there are 350 different shapes of pasta. All pasta in Italy must be made with 100 percent durum semolina, because it is the law in Italy.

Italian Specialties

Stuffed Artichokes

Serves 8

STALE BREAD ENOUGH TO MAKE 4 CUPS
4-5 TABLESPOONS PECORINO ROMANO CHEESE
8 MEDIUM ARTICHOKES
1 EGG
1/2 CUP FRESH PARSLEY
1 CLOVE GARLIC
2 TEASPOONS OLIVE OIL
SALT AND PEPPER TO TASTE

1. Shred the bread until it looks like crumbs.
2. Add the pecorino romano cheese to taste.
3. Cut up parsley and garlic.
4. Salt and pepper to taste.
5. Blend all dry ingredients.
6. Add the egg and 1 teaspoon of olive oil; blend and stir all the ingredients. Set aside.
7. Cut off all the tips of artichoke leaves, top and bottom; strip off bottom leaves.
8. Wash artichokes, and spread rows of leaves.
9. Place stuffing between the rows and the center of the artichoke.
10. Use a pot big enough to hold all artichokes upright in 6–7 inches of water. Salt and add about 1 tablespoon of olive oil.
11. Cook until tender, about 20–30 minutes. Test by tasting one of the leaves.

Put on large serving plate and serve as appetizer.

The artichoke is one of the oldest cultivated plants. In traditional European medicine, the leaves of the artichoke were used for medicinal purposes.[2] However, in our family we used the artichoke for simply the pleasure of eating.

Mini Calzone

Serves 8-10

1 PACKAGE DRY YEAST
1 CUP LUKEWARM WATER
4 CUPS FLOUR
2 TABLESPOON SUGAR
PINCH OF SALT
ONE (15-OUNCE) CONTAINER OF RICOTTA
1/2 CUP MOZZARELLA, DICED
VEGETABLE OIL FOR FRYING
2 CUPS MARINARA SAUCE (SEE PAGE 54) YOU MAY USE AS MUCH AS DESIRED

1. Dissolve yeast in water; let stand for 5 minutes.
2. In a large bowl, mix flour, sugar, and salt together.
3. Add yeast mixture, and stir until dough forms a large ball.
4. Knead for 10 minutes, adding additional flour if necessary.
5. Place dough in a greased bowl, and cover with a clean cloth; set in a draft free spot until the dough doubles in bulk.
6. Remove from bowl and knead again.
7. In a separate bowl, mix the mozzarella and the ricotta.
8. Take a small piece of dough, and stretch it into a circle with your fingers. Do this to the rest of the dough.
9. Place ricotta filling on the bottom of each circle.
10. Dip finger in lukewarm water, and rub around edge of circle. Fold top half of circle and press together. Edges can be sealed with a fork.
11. Heat vegetable oil. Place calzone in vegetable oil; brown on one side and then turn over. Calzone will rise because of the yeast.

On serving plates place the calzones in circular fashion with a small dipping bowl place some marinara sauce.

Note: If you want, you may add prosciutto, ham, or salami to the filling.

The calzone has its origin in Naples and is shaped like a half-moon. In Italy, it is stuffed with various ingredients, according to its region. Mini calzones are sold by vendors in Italy because of their ease of eating while walking.[3]

Eggplant Parmesan

Serves 10

2 EGGS
1 TABLESPOON MILK
11/2 CUPS BREAD CRUMBS, PLAIN OR SEASONED
2 EGGPLANTS, LONG AND NARROW
VEGETABLE OIL
6 CUPS MARINARA SAUCE (SEE PAGE 54)
PECORINO ROMANO CHEESE
1 POUND MOZZARELLA

1. In a round dish, add egg and 1 tablespoon milk; beat well.
2. Put the bread crumbs in flat dish.
3. Partially peel the eggplant in strips, from top to bottom.
4. Slice eggplant in 1/4-inch slices.
5. Place slices on paper towels to drain moisture. For best results, let stand about 2 hours.
6. Dip slices on both sides into beaten egg, and then coat both sides of the eggplant with the bread crumbs.
7. In a large frying pan, heat about 1 inch of vegetable oil; it must be hot and sizzling.
8. Place slices in hot oil; brown on one side and then turn over.
9. When eggplant is browned on both sides, place on paper towel.
10. In a baking pan, cover the the bottom of the baking pan with marinara sauce
11. Layer eggplant, sauce, and pecorino romano cheese; repeat as desired. Cover the last layer of the eggplant with the mozzarella and more marinara sauce.
12. Before baking the eggplant, cover with foil; this prevents drying out of eggplant.
13. Bake at 375 degrees for about 10 minutes, or until mozzarella is melted.

When cooked let sit for about 5 minutes, cut eggplant in criss-cross sections and serve

Note: If you are preparing for a large family or group, then for each added eggplant you would need to have more mozzarella, pecorino romano cheese, eggs, and bread crumbs.

There are several opinions about the origin of eggplant parmesan. One theory has it originating in Parma, Italy, because of the name. Others say a dish like eggplant parmesan would have to come from Sicily. In the mid 1800s, tomatoes became popular in Naples, and so the guess would be that eggplant parmesan as we know it comes from somewhere around Naples.[4]

Fried Zucchini or Squash

Serves 6

1 TABLESPOON MILK
EGGS AS NEEDED
BREAD CRUMBS, PLAIN OR SEASONED AS NEEDED
2 LARGE ZUCCHINI OR SQUASH
VEGETABLE OIL
MARINARA SAUCE AS NEEDED (SEE PAGE 54)

1. In a dish, add eggs and 1 tablespoon milk; beat well.
2. Put the bread crumbs in a flat dish.
3. Slice zucchini/squash into 1/4-inch slices.
4. Pat the zucchini/squash with paper towels to get water out.
5. Dip the slices of the zucchini on both sides into beaten eggs; then coat both sides of the zucchini with the bread crumbs.
6. In a frying pan, heat about an inch of oil until it is hot and sizzling.
7. Place slices into hot vegetable oil.
8. Brown on one side before turning over.
9. When both sides are browned, place on paper towel.

When excess oil is drained place on serving plate, if desired add marinara sauce to a dipping bowl.

Squash, unlike many of the recipes in this book, did not have its origin in Italy. Squash has its history in the Americas. Centuries after its use in the Americas, Italians developed a variety of squash, now called zucchini. The zucchini has a delicate flavor and requires little more than quick cooking with butter and olive oil. In Italy, zucchini are served in a variety of ways: in the pan, in the oven, boiled, and fried. They are served alone or in combinations with a variety of other ingredients.[5]

Frittata with Spaghetti

Serves 6

4–6 EGGS, OR AS FEW OR AS MANY AS YOU WANT
2–3 TABLESPOONS OLIVE OIL
MINCED GARLIC CLOVE
MINCED ONION
LEFTOVER SPINACH, OR ANY OTHER VEGETABLE
LEFTOVER PEPPERS
LEFTOVER SPAGHETTI

1. Scramble eggs and set aside.
2. In a frying pan, heat olive oil; add garlic and onion, and sauté in a skillet.
3. Add pepper and spinach; stir together.
4. Add leftover spaghetti; mix together.
5. When hot, add eggs and cover.
6. When all seems to stick together, take a plate larger than the frying pan, and turn frittata onto plate.
7. Now slide frittata back onto the frying pan, and continue cooking until done.

When cooked serve immediately.

Note: This recipe may be used with any other type of pasta.

A frittata is a good way to use up leftovers in your refrigerator—for example, leftover spaghetti, broccoli, boiled potatoes, and spinach.

The frittata is a homestyle meal. Very rarely will you find a restaurant that makes frittatas. Aunt Mil used to make the frittata to get her son to eat vegetables that he didn't like.

Peas à la Castrataro

Serves 4

3–4 TABLESPOONS OLIVE OIL
1 MEDIUM ONION, SLICED
4–8OUNCES MARINARA SAUCE (SEE PAGE 54)
BASIL
3–5 TEASPOONS GARLIC SALT
PEAS, 1 LARGE CAN OR FROZEN PACKAGE
2 EGGS
PECORINO ROMANO OR PARMESAN CHEESE
1 LARGE LOAF OF FRESH ITALIAN BREAD

1. In a medium frying pan, brown onions and olive oil, but do not burn.
2. Add marinara sauce, basil, garlic salt, and 4 ounces of water; simmer about 10 minutes.
3. Add peas, and simmer another 5 minutes.
4. On medium heat, add eggs and pecorino romano or parmesan cheese. If it appears to be too thick, add some water.
5. Cook until the eggs are done.

When cooked best served in soup bowls. Cut Italian bread into desired size for dipping.

Note: If using canned peas, use the water from the canned peas. This is a quick lunch meal that is delicious.

Peppers and Eggs

Serves 4-5

2 BELL PEPPERS ANY COLOR
3–4 TABLESPOONS OLIVE OIL
GARLIC POWDER
ONION, IF DESIRED
DICED TOMATOES OR TOMATO SAUCE
4–6 EGGS
SALT
1 LARGE ITALIAN BREAD

1. 1) Wash and dry peppers; cut into 1-inch pieces.
2. 2) In a large skillet, heat olive oil. Add peppers, if desired add the onions using medium heat. Sprinkle garlic powder, and cover, stirring often.
3. 3) When peppers are soft, add 3 tablespoons tomato sauce or diced tomatoes and 2 tablespoons water. Cover and cook for about 4–5 minutes.
4. 4) Add eggs whole; separate with a fork and cover. Salt to taste. Cook until the eggs are done.

Serve on large serving tray, distribute other plates for eating. Cut Italian bread as desired.

A Little Humorous Story

Aunt Mil's mother, our grandmother, was Maria Castrataro, who was born in 1879 in a small town of about five thousand people in Sala Consilina, in the city of Salerno, Italy. Grandma had six children in Italy and then four children in America; one child died at the age of three. The other nine married and gave Grandma and Grandpa twenty-three grandchildren, which was not unusual in those days. One can imagine what it was like when her children and grandchildren visited on any given weekend without an invite, which was not unusual for Italian Americans in that era.

On most weekends and holidays, my grandparents filled the three-story house they owned in Richmond Hill, Queens, New York, from September through June, or at their bungalow in Island Park, Nassau County, New York in the summer from July through August. It was rare for fewer than thirty people to be there. Now visualize my grandmother and various other women feeding all of them at the same time, using the recipes that are in this book. You can imagine how much we kids looked forward to these meals.

Where did they put all these people? Picture a large dining room with no walls from east to west and that led right into the master bedroom—again with no walls—and then into the living room with no walls. This is sometimes referred to as railroad rooms. All this was on the second floor; tenants lived on the third floor. The first floor was rented by Aunt Mill, her husband, and their three children, which was where most of the children from the second floor went under adult supervision. The worst part of this for us children? We had to kiss every single adult before we could start to play.

Joe and I don't remember any of us kids being scolded or punished. Either we have very poor memories or it was simply the culture at the time. We do remember our parents staring at us if we were about to disobey. That's all it took—one strong stare.

As for the bungalow, everything was done in the yard and not indoors. We made sure to hear the weather forecast before going to the bungalow!

Pickled Eggplant

1 EGGPLANT
2–3 CLOVES GARLIC
1 CUP VINEGAR
JAR FOR SEALING

1. Slice eggplant into 1 × 4–inch long strips.
2. Blanch in boiling water 1–2 minutes. See below.
3. Strain water out.
4. Put eggplant strips and chopped garlic cloves in a jar.
5. Fill jar with vinegar. Seal jar with a cover.

Note: Recipes sometimes call for cooks to "blanch" fruits or vegetables. All it means is to put the item in question in boiling water, lift it out after the prescribed time, and cool it off quickly.[6]

Pizza di Grano—Italian Cheese Grain Pie

1 CUP WHOLE-GRAIN HULLED WHEAT; SOAK
FOR 1 DAY IN THE REFRIGERATOR
FOR PASTRY
3 CUPS SIFTED ALL-PURPOSE FLOUR
6 TABLESPOONS BUTTER
6 TABLESPOONS LARD
1 EGG YOLK, BEATEN; RESERVE THE WHITE FOR FILLING
ABOUT 1/2 CUP COLD WATER
1 1/2 TABLESPOONS SUGAR
1 TABLESPOON SALT

For Filling

1 CUP MILK
1 CUP HEAVY CREAM
2 SLICES LEMON RIND; NO WHITE PART
1/4 TEASPOON SALT
1/4 CUP LIGHT BROWN SUGAR, PACKED
PINCH OF CINNAMON
3/4 CUP SUGAR
3 EGGS, SEPARATED
1 POUND RICOTTA
1 TABLESPOON GRATED LEMON PEEL
1/2 CUP OF SUGAR FOR THE EGG WHITES
1/4 CUP CANDIED CITRON, FIRMLY CHOPPED

For Pastry

1. Place flour in large mixing bowl. Cut in butter and lard with pastry blender or knife and fork.
2. Add sugar, salt, and the beaten egg yolk with 1 tablespoon of cold water.
3. Using a fork or your fingertips, work the egg yolk into the mixture.
4. Add the rest of the water a little at a time.
5. Divide into thirds: 2 for the bottom and 1 for a lattice top.
6. Roll bottom into 11-inch round for 9-inch pie plate; trim along the edge of plate.

For Filling

1. Drain wheat, and put it in a pot with about 4 cups of cold water. Bring water to a boil; simmer for about 1 hour. Drain.
2. Place wheat in saucepan with milk, cream, lemon rind, brown sugar, cinnamon, and salt. Over moderate heat, bring to a boil; then reduce heat and simmer for 20 minutes. Discard the lemon rind, and let it cool.
3. In a large mixing bowl, with electric mixer at medium speed, mix 3/4 cup sugar and egg yolks; beat until light lemon colored.
4. Add ricotta, citron, grated lemon peel, and cooled grain mixture.
5. In a separate bowl, beat 4 egg whites, adding 1/2 cup of sugar slowly, until mixture stands in firm peaks.
6. Gently fold (see note below) into the grain-ricotta mixture.
7. Spoon mixture into the shells.
8. To make lattice top, roll out the reserved dough, and cut into 1/2-inch strips. Fashion into lattice top, allowing 3/4 inch between strips. Moisten ends of the strips to make them stick.
9. Heat oven to 350 degrees. Cook for 1 hour, or until center is set and the color is a light tan. Remove from oven and chill.
10. 10) Serve with confectioner's sugar on top.

Note: Though the name is Pizza di Grano, it is a pie that is traditionally served only at Easter time. When Pizza di Grano is made properly, it is something you will look forward to every Easter.

Gently fold. When you combine beaten egg whites with other heavier mixtures, handle carefully so you don't lose the air you've beaten into the whites. It's best to pour the heavier mixture onto the beaten egg whites.[7]

Pizza Dough

Makes 1 large pie

1 PACKAGE OF ACTIVE DRY YEAST
2 CUPS WARM WATER
1 TEASPOON SALT
1 EGG, BEATEN
1 TEASPOON COOKING OIL
5–6 CUPS UNBLEACHED WHITE FLOUR
MARINARA SAUCE (SEE PAGE 54)
MOZZARELLA, SLICED THIN OR DICED

1. In a large mixing bowl, dissolve yeast in warm water.
2. Add salt, egg, cooking oil, and 4 cups of flour to the yeast and water. Stir thoroughly.
3. Turn dough out onto floured board, and continue kneading while adding flour until dough is smooth and elastic.
4. Return dough to bowl, and place in a warm, draft-free place; cover and let it rise for about 1 1/2 hours, or until the dough has doubled in size.
5. Punch down place onto floured board, and cut into 2–3 pieces, depending on the size of the pizza pan.
6. Pat and stretch the dough to fit on pan.
7. Grease pans lightly with oil, and place dough on pan.
8. Ladle the marinara sauce on the dough; cover the sauce with mozzarella and (if desired) with your choice of toppings.
9. Heat oven to 450 degrees. Cook for 30 minutes, or until crust is crisp.

Pizza Rustica

Serves 6 - 8

2 CUPS RICOTTA
1 CUP MOZZARELLA
1 1/2 CUPS COOKED RICE
4 HARD-BOILED EGGS
2 EGGS, BEATEN
1/2 CUP ITALIAN SALAMI, DICED
1/2 CUP DRIED ITALIAN SAUSAGE, DICED
1/2 CUP SOPPRESSATA, DICED
1/4 CUP PROSCIUTTO, DICED
6–8 TABLESPOONS PECORINO ROMANO OR PARMESAN CHEESE
PIE DOUGH (SEE PIZZA DOUGH RECIPE, PAGE 36)

1. In a large mixing bowl, combine all ingredients, stirring gently. It's best mixed with hands.
2. Spread mixed ingredients evenly into 2–3 pie-dough shells, depending on how high you want the filling.
3. Preheat oven to 350 degrees. Bake 40–45 minutes, until surface is set and a toothpick inserted in the center comes out clean.
4. Allow to cool before serving.

Cut into desired size slices and serve

Note: Pizza Rustica is another traditional Italian Easter pie. It's absolutely delicious and is meant to not only celebrate Easter but also celebrate the ending of Lent. Many traditional Italian Catholics gave up meat for lent. Pizza Rustica was to be part of their festive celebration at Easter.[8]

Pizza Rustica, also known as Italian Easter pie, is a time-honored Italian tradition. As the name states, this pie is only made at Easter. This is a delicious dish that celebrated the end of Lent and the holiday of Easter.[8]

Potato Pancakes à la Castrataro

Serves 4 for every 4 potatoes

**POTATOES, MASHED WITH BUTTER AND MILK (NUMBER
OF POTATOES IS BASED ON FAMILY SIZE)
3–4 SPRIGS OF PARSLEY, LEAVES CHOPPED
1 EGG SCRAMBLED FOR EVERY 4 POTATOES
PECORINO ROMANO GRATING CHEESE
1/4 CUP FLOUR
1/4 CUP OLIVE OIL FOR FRYING**

1. In a large pot, boil potatoes. When cooked, mash the potatoes and place in refrigerator overnight.
2. Put cold mashed potatoes in a large bowl.
3. Mix in the chopped parsley leaves.
4. Add egg and pecorino romano cheese to taste, mixing all ingredients well.
5. Dip your hands in flour so the mixture does not stick to your hands. Add 1 tablespoon of potatoes, forming an egg-shaped pancake.
6. Dip pancake into flour so stickiness disappears; put on plate. Continue this until all potato mixture is used up.
7. Heat olive oil in a frying pan. Add pancakes, and cook until they are light brown.
8. When cooked, place on paper towels. They may be served hot or cold.

Potatoes Roasted

Serves 4

4–6 POTATOES, DEPENDING ON SIZE
3 ONIONS
3 TABLESPOONS OLIVE OIL
TOMATOES, DICED (OPTIONAL)
OREGANO (OPTIONAL)

1. If potatoes are large, cut into eighths; if they're small, cut into quarters.
2. Cut onions into either quarters or eighths.
3. Place potatoes in roasting pan; sprinkle olive oil on top.
4. Preheat oven to 375 degrees. Add potatoes, and cook for 10 minutes.
5. Turn potatoes over, and add onions. Sprinkle on oregano, and add diced tomatoes if desired.
6. Continue to bake until potatoes are brown.

String Beans in Tomato Sauce

Serves 4

3–4 TABLESPOONS OLIVE OIL
2 CLOVES GARLIC, CHOPPED
3–4 PLUM TOMATOES, DICED
SALT
1 CUP WATER
1 POUND STRING BEANS, CLEANED AND CUT BITE SIZE
BASIL LEAVES
1 MEDIUM LOAF ITALIAN BREAD

1. In a medium skillet, heat olive oil on medium heat; add garlic to taste and brown it, but do not burn.
2. Add tomatoes, and sauté for 10–15 minutes. Add salt to taste. Stir, but do not burn.
3. Add 1 cup of water, and simmer for 5 minutes.
4. Add string beans and basil. Cook until tender.

Serve in soup bowls and cut Italian bread in slices for dipping.

Note: This makes a delicious meatless meal by using more of the above ingredients plus 2–3 diced potatoes, which will be added at the same time as the beans.

The green bean was first grown in Central and South America. When Columbus returned from his trips to the Americas, he introduced the green bean to the Mediterranean region. Over the years in Italy, various recipes were made using the green bean. Aunt Mil's recipe for green beans is one of these recipes.[9]

Squash Castrataro Style

Serves 4-6

2–3 TABLESPOONS OLIVE OIL
1 GARLIC CLOVE
1 (8-OUNCE) CAN OF DEL MONTE SAUCE
1/2 TEASPOON SALT
3–4 BASIL LEAVES
1–2 SQUASH, DEPENDING ON SIZE
2 EGGS
2–3 TABLESPOONS PECORINO ROMANO GRATING CHEESE
1 MEDIUM ITALIAN BREAD

1. In a medium sauce pan, put in olive oil and heat. Add garlic, but do not burn it; remove garlic.
2. Add can of tomato sauce, basil leaves, salt, and 1 can of water. Bring to a boil, lower the heat, and simmer for 10 minutes.
3. Add squash. When you add the squash, you may need to add some more water to keep the sauce juicy so that it doesn't dry up when you add the eggs and pecorino romano cheese. Cook for 10 minutes.
4. Add whole eggs and stir, breaking up the eggs with a fork. Add cheese, and stir with a fork.

Best served in soup bowl. Cut Italian bread into slices for dipping.

Tomato Salad and Bruschetta

Serves 8- 10 depending on the number of tomatoes

6–10 PLUM TOMATOES
1 ONION
1 CLOVE GARLIC
BASIL LEAVES
OLIVE OIL
ITALIAN BREAD, AS NEEDED
SALT TO TASTE

1. Dice the tomatoes, onions, garlic, and basil leaves.
2. Put all the ingredients in a salad bowl.
3. Sprinkle the ingredients with olive oil, and add 1 tablespoon water. Salt to taste, toss with fork, and spoon to mix it. Add olives.
4. Cut italian bread into bite-size slices, and then toast.
5. Set the toasted italian bread up on tray or large dish; add the bruschetta on top of it.

Bruschetta is an antipasto from Tuscany, Italy, and it was originally the poor man's answer to garlic bread. It was made by toasting the bread and sprinkling garlic powder on the bread. Somewhere around 1990, restaurants started serving bruschetta with tomatoes, fresh basil, olive oil, and garlic.[10]

Gravy/Sauce

Chicken Sauce

Serves 4-6 depending on the amount of chicken used

4-6 CHICKEN PARTS LEGS THIGHS BREASTS CAN BE USED
2 GARLIC CLOVES CHOPPED OR DICED
1 LARGE CAN PLUM TOMATOES
1 CAN TOMATO PASTE
BASIL

1. In a large, deep nonstick skillet, brown the pieces of chicken until cooked. Set aside and keep warm.
2. Add garlic to chicken drippings; cook until brown, but do not burn it.
3. Dice the plum tomatoes, and then add tomatoes and juice of tomatoes. Cook 30 minutes.
4. Add paste and basil, blending everything; add a paste can of water.
5. Add cooked chicken, and continue cooking on low heat for about an hour. Keep adding water a little at a time.

Best served with spaghetti.

Note: Chicken sauce will be lighter and thinner than meat sauce.

Marinara Sauce

Serves 4-6

2–3 CLOVES GARLIC
OLIVE OIL
2 CANS PLUM TOMATOES
1 CAN TOMATO PASTE
1 BASIL SPRIG

1. In a large skillet, heat oil then add garlic, and sauté.
2. Before adding plum tomatoes, dice them and throw away tops, if attached. Add tomatoes and the juice of the tomatoes. Cook on low heat about 30 minutes.
3. Add paste and basil, blending everything. Add 2 paste cans of water. Cook on medium heat for about 30 minutes so that the tomatoes stay chunky.

Serve with any form of pasta

Around 1550, Spain occupied the region of Naples, Italy, thus introducing tomatoes to this region. As a result, marinara sauce was developed, becoming popular in this region almost two hundred years earlier than the rest of Europe. Marinara sauce is the most basic of the Italian sauces. It can be combined with a wide variety of spices to create different flavors.[11]

Meat Sauce

Serves 6-8 with leftovers

3 TABLESPOONS OLIVE OIL
PORK OR BEEF NECK BONES
1POUND SAUSAGE SWEET OR HOT
BRACIOLE (SEE RECIPE PAGE 62)
MEATBALLS (SEE RECIPE PAGE 68)
PIECE BOTTOM ROUND
2 GLOVES GARLIC, CHOPPED
3 28 OUNCE CANS TOMATOES
1 SMALL TOMATO PASTE
BASIL

1. In a large pot, heat the olive oil on medium heat. Add the neck bones, turning occasionally to brown on all sides. Remove the neck bones from the pot.
2. Place the sausage in the same pot, turning and browning on all sides. Remove the sausage from the pot.
3. If bottom round or other raw meats are desired, follow the same directions as above.
4. Add garlic to meat drippings. Cook until brown, but do not burn.
5. Add tomatoes to drippings; cook until all water seems to be gone.
6. Add tomato paste, and blend well.
7. Add basil, stirring into sauce.
8. Add two tomato cans of water, stirring well.
9. Add the cooked meats into the sauce. Cook on low heat for about an hour and a half, or until meat is tender. Stir sauce every now and then.
10. If sauce begins to get too thick, add water a little at a time.

Tips

1. Put the meatballs in the sauce pot for 10 minutes before serving—or better still, put them in a separate pot with some sauce.
2. When adding water, if amount is not given, use your discretion so sauce doesn't get too thick.

Note: The amount of meats used depends on the size of the family. If you do not wish to use all the meats, you can choose which ones you want.

In Italy, a meat sauce is commonly called ragu. There are fourteen different types of ragu. The common denominator among these varieties is they are all made with meat, and they are used with pasta. In Northern Italy, the meat sauce is minced and chopped and then sautéed with vegetables. Any type meat may be used, and the liquid used may be broth, milk, water, or wine. In Southern Italy, the ragu is made with whole cuts of beef, pork, and sausage, which is then added to the tomatoes.[12]

Shrimp Sauce

Serves 4

2–3 TABLESPOONS OLIVE OIL
2–3 CLOVES GARLIC
BASIL LEAVES
1 28OUNCE CAN OF TOMATOES, DICED OR CHOPPED
1 CAN TOMATO PASTE
1POUND SHRIMP, CLEANED AND DEVEINED
1POUND SPAGHETTI

1. If the shrimp are extra-large or jumbo, cut them in half.
2. In a large skillet, heat olive oil and garlic, but do not burn.
3. Add tomatoes and basil. Cook over medium heat, and salt to taste. Stir to prevent sticking and burning of tomatoes. Cover.
4. After about 15 minutes, add 1 cup water and 1–2 teaspoons tomato paste. Stir, and cook for 15–20 minutes.
5. This is to be a light fish sauce, so if it is too thick, add some water, and then add the shrimp. Cook until shrimp turn pink, stir, and shut off heat; do not overcook the shrimp.
6. In a large pot bring 5 quarts of water to a boil, add salt to taste, a drop of olive oil to keep pasta from sticking together. Cook according to direction on box.

Place pasta in a large serving dish then add shrimp sauce and stir together. Use flat plates to serve food on.

Meats

Braciole

Serves 4-5

2 1/2 CUPS STALE ITALIAN BREAD
3 SPRIGS FRESH PARSLEY, CHOPPED
1/2 CUP PECORINO ROMANO CHEESE
1 GARLIC GLOVE, DICED
1 EGG
OLIVE OIL
2 1/2 POUNDS TOP SIRLOIN, CUBED CHUCK, OR SIRLOIN STEAK
THREAD OR BAKERY CORD, FOR TYING

1. In a large mixing bowl, shred the bread until it looks like crumbs.
2. Add the pecorino romano cheese, parsley, and garlic to taste.
3. Salt and pepper to taste. Mix all the ingredients.
4. Add egg and 1 teaspoon of olive oil; blend and stir all ingredients.
5. Whichever meat you choose, slice it thin and pound the meat flat.
6. Put stuffing on top of the meat, and roll the meat over the stuffing.
7. Tie the roll from one end to the other so that it holds in the stuffing.
8. Fry in hot olive oil, browning on all sides.

This recipe is made for the inclusion in a meat sauce on page 56.

Braciole is the American name of an Italian dish usually made with beef or pork. In Italy, it is called *involtini*. In different regions of Italy, fish and chicken may be substituted for the pork or beef.[13] Try it using the braciole recipe.

Chicken à la Castrataro

Serves 4

1 CHICKEN, CUT UP IN BITE SIZES; WASHED AND DRIED
SALT
OLIVE OIL
2–3 EGGS
4–5 TABLESPOONS PARSLEY
5 TABLESPOONS GRATED CHEESE
2 LEMONS
2–3 TABLESPOONS LEMON JUICE

1. Coat the bottom of a large frying pan with some olive oil.
2. Heat to warm, and then add chicken and cover. Sauté in medium to high heat, stirring and turning the pieces until brown on all sides. Salt to taste.
3. In a bowl, mix eggs, parsley, cheese, lemon juice, and the juice and pulp of the fresh lemons.
4. When the chicken is cooked, lower the heat, and pour the egg mixture over the chicken. Stir the eggs to cover all the pieces of the chicken. Salt to taste.
5. Raise heat again, and stir. When egg mixture is cooked, set aside and allow it to cool.
6. Place in a covered container and store in the refrigerator.

Note: This is best eaten cold.

Chicken Cacciatore

Serves 4

1 CUT-UP CHICKEN
1 POUND MUSHROOMS, SLICED OR DICED
4–5 TOMATOES, DICED
BASIL LEAVES
SALT AND PEPPER
1 POUND SPAGHETTI
OLIVE OIL

1. Brown chicken in large frying pan on medium heat; if necessary, use some olive oil to prevent sticking.
2. When chicken is almost cooked, add mushrooms so that they will brown.
3. Add tomatoes, basil, and salt and pepper to taste. Cover on low heat, and cook for about 20 minutes.
4. In a large pot, add salt to taste, and boil water. When water boils, add spaghetti and cook per the box directions.

When cooked place the spaghetti in a large serving dish and cover with the chicken cacciatore and serve on smaller plates.

Cacciatore means hunter in Italian. This dish originated somewhere around the sixteenth century. It was a dish for the wealthy because they were the only ones who could enjoy the sport of hunting. Though the word means hunter, it was actually used to simply remember the members of the Cacciatore family, who have been cooking in this region for more than one thousand years.[14]

Meatballs

Serves 6

STALE ITALIAN BREAD, OR 4–5 SLICES WHITE BREAD
1–2 GARLIC CLOVES, MINCED
ONION, MINCED
1–2 EGGS
3–4 SPRIGS PARSLEY, DICED
1/4–1/2 CUP PECORINO ROMANO CHEESE
1POUND MEAT CHUCK CHOP
OLIVE OIL

1. If you use italian bread, soak it in water and then squeeze out the water completely. With the white bread, cut top crust off and then shred it; do not moisten yet.
2. Add all ingredients to the bread in a bowl, except the meat and olive oil, and mix well.
3. Add the meat in little lumps so that it will mix well to the bread mixture. Add 1–2 teaspoons olive oil.
4. Hand roll meat into balls; the size is up to you.
5. In a large frying pan, cook using hot olive oil.

When cooked, if you plan on adding meatballs to your meat sauce(see page 56), do it about 10 minutes before you are ready to serve them, or else they will soak up all your sauce. Even better, put the meatballs in a smaller pot with some sauce, thus preserving the rest of the sauce. Meatballs can also be served without sauce.

No one knows from where the meatball actually originated. Meatballs were known in Asia, the Middle East, North Africa, and parts of Europe. When Italian immigrants came to America, they brought with them their own meatball recipes, many of which evolved according to family tradition.[15] In our book we offer two different meatball recipes, both over one hundred years old, handed down from different families. Bon appetit!

Meatballs with Raisins

Serves 12

1 LOAF STALE WHEAT BREAD
2 ONIONS, CHOPPED AND DICED
3 POUNDS CHOP MEAT
2 PACKETS OF LIPTON ONION SOUP MIX
1 LARGE BOWL OF WATER
3 EGGS
2 TABLESPOONS PARSLEY, CHOPPED
1 REGULAR SIZE BOX OF WHITE RAISINS
3/4 CUP BREAD CRUMBS
OLIVE OIL, FOR FRYING

1. Cut the crust off the whole-wheat bread. Break apart, and soak the entire loaf.
2. Squeeze the water out of bread; bread should be wet but not soggy. Place it in a bowl.
3. Sautee the onions in olive oil, until lightly browned. Drain the onions.
4. Add all the ingredients in the bowl with the whole-wheat bread. Make sure to thoroughly mix the ingredients.
5. In the cup of your hand, take the ingredients, roll, and make small meatballs. Put in frying pan with 1/2 cup olive oil.
6. Brown the meatballs on all sides, and transfer them to a cookie sheet. Cover with aluminum foil. Heat oven to 375 degrees. Add meatballs in the oven for 45 minutes.

Note: If you're adding meatballs to meat sauce (see page 56), do it right before serving.

In Italy, many families used different ingredients in their meatball recipes, and it did not matter which region of Italy they were from. This recipe has been handed down from another family, and it is at least one hundred years old. Try it you will love it!

Meatloaf

Serves 4

HARD ITALIAN BREAD, OR 4–5 SLICES OF STALE WHITE BREAD
1 ONION, CHOPPED
FRESH PARSLEY
GARLIC
PECORINO ROMANO CHEESE
1–2 EGGS
1 POUND CHOPPED MEAT
1–2 TEASPOONS OLIVE OIL

1. If using the white bread, cut the top crust off and then shred.
2. If you use italian bread, soak in water and then squeeze out all the water completely. With the white bread, just shred and do not moisten yet.
3. Add all the dry ingredients to the bread in a bowl.
4. Add the eggs and mix well.
5. Add the meat in little lumps so that it will mix well to the bread.
6. Add 1–2 teaspoons olive oil to the mixture.
7. Preheat the oven to 350 degrees.
8. Shape the meatloaf into bread shape form. Cook it in a loaf pan, casserole dish, or baking sheet. Place meatloaf in the oven, and cook for about an hour; the temperature should be about 160 degrees in the center.
9. If you desire you may brush tomato sauce to the top and sides of meatloaf in step 8.

This meal is best served with your choice of potato and vegetable.

Some types of meatloaf have been in existence since ancient times. However, modern meatloaf came into popularity after the meat grinder was invented. Meatloaf was also greatly appreciated during the Great Depression, because many Americans were able to stretch meals with the use of meatloaf.[16]

Pot Roast

Serves 6

3–4 POUNDS BOTTOM OR RUMP ROAST
1–2 LARGE ONIONS, SLICED IN ROUNDS
GARLIC POWDER
6–8 LARGE POTATOES, CUT INTO EIGHTHS
4–6 CARROTS, CUT INTO CHUNKS
1 15OUNCE CAN OR 12OUNCE PACKAGE FROZEN PEAS

1. In a covered Dutch oven pot, brown meat on all sides on medium-high heat for about 1/2 hour. It's okay if the meat looks burnt; that adds to the flavor.
2. Add onion rounds and brown the onions. Add 2–3 cups of water and garlic powder to taste. Lower heat so that meat and onions will cook together and meat will become tender; this will give it a natural gravy look. You can sprinkle garlic powder and salt on the meat to taste. Cook for about 2 hours.
3. Add potatoes and carrots; cover the vegetables with water, and let cook until tender.
4. You may add the peas to the pot roast or cook them on the side separately, in case someone does not like peas. If desired, sprinkle garlic powder.

Pot roast is a dish that originated in the United States. However, it uses a cooking style from Europe called braising. Pot roast was originally called Yankee pot roast because it came from the New England area.[17]

Chicken with Stuffing

Serves 4

ROASTING CHICKEN, ABOUT 5 POUNDS
SALT
LEMON JUICE
PARSLEY
PECORINO ROMANO CHEESE
STUFFING BREAD
1–2 GIZZARDS, MINCED
2–4 CHICKEN LIVERS, CHOPPED
GARLIC, CHOPPED
2–3 EGGS
OLIVE OIL

1. Marinate the chicken in water for at least 2 hours with salt and lemon juice.
2. In a frying pan, cook the gizzards and the liver in olive oil until tender.
3. Mix the other ingredients together, and then add the gizzards and liver.
4. Place the chicken in roasting pan. Spread butter on the outside of the chicken and in the cavity. Then shake garlic powder on the outside of the chicken.
5. Fill the cavity and the neck opening with the stuffing mixture. Then seal the cavity.
6. Cook at 350 degrees. The rule of thumb is 20 minutes per pound.
7. A whole chicken is ready when a meat thermometer inserted into the inner thigh, close to but not touching the thigh bone, reads at least 165 degrees Fahrenheit, or 74 degrees Celsius.

When cooked best served with a potato and vegetable of your choice.

Note: You may substitute the chicken with roast turkey or Cornish hen.

Roast chicken has been prepared throughout the world for millennia. In Italy, there are at least twenty-three breeds of chicken that are of Italian origin. In the United States, chicken consumption increased greatly during World War Two because beef and pork were at a shortage. In Europe, chicken consumption overtook beef and veal in 1996.[18]

Spareribs and Savoy Cabbage

The servings in this recipe depends on family size

SPARERIBS
PORK NECK BONES
SAVOY CABBAGE
PIG'S FEET
1 FRESH TOMATO, PEELED AND DICED
1 MEDIUM ONION WHITE OR YELLOW
GARLIC
SALT

1. Wash the cabbage, separating the leaves; set aside.
2. Wash the meats.
3. Cook meats in a big pot of water for about 30 minutes.
4. Throw out water, and refill the pot with clean water.
5. Continue cooking meat with diced onion, garlic, and salt for about 1–1 1/2 hours, until almost tender.
6. Add tomato and cabbage. Make sure to press cabbage down so it is covered by the water.
7. Continue cooking until everything is tender.

The amounts of meats depend on the size of the family.

Soups

Chicken Soup

Serves 8 with leftovers

4–6 STALKS OF CELERY, WITH LEAVES CUT IN 1-INCH PIECES
1 LARGE FRESH TOMATO, DICED
1 LARGE ONION, CUT UP IN PIECES
2–3 CARROTS, PEELED AND CUT IN CHUNK SIZES
1 CHICKEN, OR CHICKEN PARTS OF A WHOLE CHICKEN
SALT AND PEPPER
ANY SMALL PASTA

1. Cut the celery, tomato, onion, and carrots in small pieces.
2. In a large pot, add about 8–10 quarts of water; add chicken to a boil. Reduce heat after skimming off the fatty foam that has formed.
3. Continue cooking chicken for about 45 minutes.
4. Now add the vegetables and continue to cook. Salt and pepper to taste.
5. In about 20 minutes, take the chicken out of the pot and place in a frying pan.
6. Continue to cook the soup.
7. In a separate pot, cook the small pasta of your choice.
8. If soup is too much for a night's meal, take the amount you will be using and freeze the rest.
9. Add the small pasta (orzo, alphabets, pastina, etc.) to the amount of soup that is being used.
10. Shred some of the chicken in the frying pan, and add it to the soup. You may add it all if you desire.
11. If there is leftover chicken, and you have some leftover tomato sauce, add some basil leaves and let simmer until chicken absorbs some of the sauce. If it becomes too thick, add some water.

Escarole Soup

Serves 6

1–2 LARGE HEADS OF ESCAROLE
SALT
1 LARGE ONION, CUT IN PIECES
4–6 STALKS OF CELERY, WITH LEAVES CUT IN 1-INCH PIECES
1 FRESH TOMATO, DICED
3 CARROTS, PEELED AND CUT IN CHUNK SIZES

1. Wash escarole in a strainer, or by hand, leaf by leaf to be sure all the sand is washed out.
2. Bring 3–4 quarts of water to a boil. Add some salt to taste, and add escarole into the boiling water. Keep turning until all escarole is covered by the water.
3. Let escarole cook for about 15 minutes. Reduce heat, and then add all the vegetables. Cover and let simmer for about 20 minutes, or until vegetables are tender.
4. If you desire, you may add some medium-sized egg noodles that are cooked separately.

Note: Soup is best served with pecorino romano cheese sprinkled on top.

Lentil Soup with Pasta/ Pasta e Lenticchie

Serves 4

1/2–1 PACKAGE LENTILS
4–5 TABLESPOONS OLIVE OIL
2–3 CLOVES OF GARLIC
1 ONION, SLICED
2 DICED TOMATOES, OR 1 (8-OUNCE) CAN OF TOMATO SAUCE
SALT AND PEPPER
SMALL PASTA

1. Soak the lentils in water for about 1/2 hour.
2. Rinse the lentils well and check for little specks of shells.
3. On stove top, at medium heat, cook the lentils in medium pan with enough water to allow for evaporation.
4. In a frying pan on medium heat, place the olive oil and heat, and then add garlic and sliced onion; sauté them but do not burn.
5. Add tomatoes and 8 ounces of water; use salt and pepper to taste. Lower heat, and allow to simmer for about 30 minutes.
6. When sauce is done, add it to the lentil pot.
7. Use small pasta such as orzo, tubettini, or thin spaghetti broken into pieces. Cook pasta separately, and then combine with lentils.

Lentil soup

Lentils have been in existence since biblical times. Esau gave his birthright away for a lentil dish. The plains of Castellucio in Umbria are known for their production of the most famous lentils in Italy. Lentils are most popular in Italian homes on New Year's Eve. Lentil soup is made, and then at the stroke of midnight on the new year, the lentil soup is served for good luck. Lentils are very good nutritionally because they are high in vitamins and fiber.

Pasta e Fagioli

Serves 4

3 GARLIC CLOVES CHOPPED
3 TABLESPOONS OLIVE OIL
1 6-8 OUNCE CAN TOMATO PASTE
1 (15 1/2 OUNCE) CAN WHITE CANNELLINI BEANS
SALT AND PEPPER TO TASTE
ANY SMALL PASTA

1. In a large pot on medium heat, sauté the garlic until lightly brown.
2. Add tomato paste, and stir until mixed with olive oil and garlic.
3. Add the can of cannellini beans plus 3 1/2 cans of water, measured in the cannellini can. Salt and pepper to taste
4. Bring to a boil, stirring often. Simmer for 15 minutes.
5. In a separate pot, boil small pasta (orzo, alphabets, pastina,etc.) to taste.
6. Drain the small pasta, and slowly add it to the soup mixture, so you can judge the amount of pasta to add.

This recipe makes about 55 ounces of soup. Should you desire more, double the ingredients.

Pasta e fagioli is the most prevalent soup and is also the national dish of Italy. It is present in all regions of Italy. The bean, as well as tomatoes used in the soup, arrived in regions of Italy in the 1500s. The benefits of eating pasta and beans, besides the great taste, is the sense of feeling full, which is given by the fibers and fats. Legumes have always been known as the poor man's meat. Also, the legumes used, like all beans, are extremely healthy.[19]

Split Pea Soup

Serves 4

1 PACKAGE DRIED PEAS
4 BEEF FRANKS, OR A HAMBONE WITH HAM
1 LARGE ONION, CHOPPED
3–4 CARROTS, PEELED AND SLICED THIN
1 RIPE TOMATO, PEELED AND DICED
SALT AND PEPPER

1. Soak the dried peas in water for 30 minutes before using.
2. Cook the peas on medium heat. If using a hambone, add it in a large pot with 8 quarts of water. Cook for about 30 minutes.
3. Add the vegetables, and continue cooking for at least another hour.
4. If using frankfurters instead of hambone, slice them and add the frankfurters 30 minutes after adding the vegetables.

Note: The frankfurters are added after cooking the vegetables for 30 minutes

Cakes
Cookies
Pies
Tarts

Anisette Knots

Serves 15

3 1/2 CUPS ALL-PURPOSE FLOUR
PINCH OF SALT
2 TABLESPOONS BAKING POWDER
3 EGGS
3/4 CUP SUGAR
1/4 POUND MELTED BUTTER
3 TEASPOONS PURE ANISE EXTRACT
1/4 CUP WARM WATER

For Glaze

3 CUPS SIFTED CONFECTIONERS' SUGAR
3 TABLESPOONS MILK
2 TABLESPOONS PURE ANISE EXTRACT
COLORED NONPAREIL CANDY

1. In a large mixing bowl, combine flour, baking powder, salt, eggs, and sugar. Mix well; mixture will be crumbly.
2. Add melted butter, 3 teaspoons pure anise extract, and warm water. Stir until mixture forms a ball.
3. Transfer dough to a lightly floured surface, and knead for 5 minutes or until dough is smooth.
4. Chill for about 1 hour.
5. Pinch off pieces of dough that are the size of walnuts and roll into logs. Then tie each piece into a knot shape. Place on a lightly greased baking pan.
6. Heat oven to 400 degrees. Bake knots in oven for 8–10 minutes, or until bottoms are lightly brown. Cool on rack.

For Glaze. In a bowl, add confectioners' sugar, 3 tablespoons milk, and 2 tablespoons pure anise extract. Dip cookies upside down into the glaze. Turn cookies right side up, and dry over wax paper for 1 minute. Add sprinkles with nonpareils.

Biscotti Regina Cookies with Sesame Seed

Makes about 15 cookies

1/4 POUND SESAME SEEDS
2 CUPS FLOUR
1 TEASPOON BAKING POWDER
1/4 TEASPOON SALT
1/2 CUP SUGAR
1/2 CUP OIL, LARD, OR MARGARINE
2 EGGS
MILK FOR DIPPING COOKIES

1. Toast sesame (see below) seeds about 15 minutes. If you prefer, you can use sesame seeds without toasting.
2. Mix flour, baking powder, and salt together.
3. In a large bowl, beat together sugar and lard. Add eggs one at a time, while mixing.
4. Add flour mixture slowly.
5. Take a piece of the dough, and roll it into a rope shape about 1 inch in diameter. Cut into 1 1/2–2 inch pieces.
6. Place the sesame seeds on wax paper or long plate. Dip each cookie into a saucer of milk, and dip it into the seeds.
7. Place the cookies on a cookie sheet and bake at 400 degrees, until light golden brown, about 12–15 minutes.

Note: You may toast the sesame seed in a skillet for about 3–5 minutes, or you may bake them in the oven at 375 degrees until lightly browned.

Brown-Edge Butter Cookies

Makes about 95 cookies

1 1/4 CUPS SIFTED FLOUR
1/4 TEASPOON SALT
2 STICKS BUTTER, ROOM TEMPERATURE
1 CUP SUGAR
1 TEASPOON VANILLA EXTRACT
2 EGGS, ROOM TEMPERATURE

1. In a medium bowl, sift flour and salt together; set aside.
2. Cream the butter, and add the sugar; blend together. See instructions below
3. Add vanilla extract and eggs; beat until light and fluffy.
4. Add flour mixture, slowly; mixing until smooth and blended.
5. Place about 1/2 teaspoon of mixture onto an ungreased cookie sheet, about 3 inches apart. Cookies spread while baking.
6. Heat oven to 350 degrees. Bake until edges of the cookies turn light brown, about 6–8 minutes; watch them carefully.
7. Remove cookies from pan to allow them to cool.

Note: These cookies can keep for weeks in an airtight tin can, when placed in a cool place.

Note: When a recipe tells you to cream butter and sugar, it means that you should beat the two ingredients with a wooden spoon and a bit of elbow grease until they form a light, uniform, and creamy mixture. Once sugar and butter are properly creamed, the sugar crystals will have dissolved, resulting in a smooth texture.[21]

Cheesecake

Serves 6-8

2 TABLESPOONS BUTTER OR SHORTENING
4 (8-OUNCE) PACKAGES OF CREAM CHEESE
6 EGGS
1 CUP GRANULATED SUGAR
1/4 TEASPOON SALT
1/2 TEASPOON LEMON EXTRACT
1 1/2 TEASPOON VANILLA EXTRACT

1. Prepare 9-inch springform pan. Grease the bottom and sides with 2 tablespoons butter or shortening. Wrap the pan in aluminum foil so that it is watertight.
2. In a large mixing bowl, beat the cream cheese until soft.
3. Add eggs, one at a time, beating well after each addition.
4. Slowly add sugar, salt, lemon extract, and vanilla extract.
5. In a pan that is large enough to hold the springform pan, place a clean cloth and then add hot water 1/2 inch deep.
6. Place springform pan into the larger pan.
7. Place pan in 325-degree oven and bake for 1 hour.
8. Remove from oven to cooling rack, away from draft, until cake is cool.

Note: A springform pan is a type of bakeware that features sides that can be removed from the base. Springform refers to the construction style of this pan. The base and the sides are separate pieces that are held together when the base is aligned with a groove that rings the bottom of the walls. The pan is then secured by a latch on the exterior of the wall. This tightens the "belt" that becomes the walls of the pan and secures the base into the groove at the base of the walls.[20]

Coffee Cake

Serves 6-8

1/2 CUP BUTTER OR MARGARINE
1 CUP SUGAR
2 UNBEATEN EGGS
1 CUP SOUR CREAM
1 TEASPOON VANILLA EXTRACT
1 TEASPOON BAKING POWDER
2 CUPS SIFTED ALL-PURPOSE FLOUR
1 TEASPOON BAKING SODA
1/2 TEASPOON SALT

For Cake Topping

2/3 CUP LIGHT BROWN SUGAR, FIRMLY PACKED
2 TABLESPOONS BUTTER OR MARGARINE, MELTED
1 CUP PECANS OR WALNUTS, CHOPPED
1 TABLESPOON CINNAMON (OPTIONAL)

1. In a small mixing bowl, mix the topping ingredients together. Be sure to blend well. Set aside.
2. Now start on the cake mix. Cream butter and sugar together until light and fluffy.
3. Add eggs, sour cream, and vanilla extract; beat well.
4. Sift together, flour, baking powder, baking soda, and salt.
5. Add them to the cream mixture, blending well.
6. Spoon 1/4 of the mixture into a well-greased, 9-inch square baking pan.
7. Sprinkle on half the topping mixture. Spoon in the remaining cake mixture.
8. Sprinkle on the remaining topping mixture, and bake at 350 degrees for 40–45 minutes, or until the cake is done.

Note: When a recipe tells you to cream butter and sugar, it means that you should beat the two ingredients with a wooden spoon and a bit of elbow grease until they form a light, uniform, and creamy mixture. Once sugar and butter are properly creamed, the sugar crystals will have dissolved, resulting in a smooth texture.[21]

Crostoli

Servings 30 depending on the size you make

2 CUPS FLOUR
1/4 TEASPOON SALT
3 EGGS
1/2 TABLESPOON VANILLA EXTRACT
1/4–1/2 CUP ICING SUGAR
TINY RAINBOW SPRINKLES (CIRCLE)

1. Put 1 cup of flour and salt into a medium bowl. Make a well in the center, adding 1 egg at a time, and mix slightly after each addition. Add vanilla extract. Stir in more of the flour to make a soft dough.
2. Turn dough onto a floured surface, and knead until dough is smooth and elastic. Cover and let stand to breathe for about 30 minutes.
3. Divide into halves or quarters. Lightly roll each section into a rectangle approximately 1/4–1/2 inches thick. Cut into 2- to 4-inch strips. Using the palm of your hands, roll to pencil thickness. Cut into 2- to 4- inch pieces and shape into bowties.
4. Fill a deep frying pan with oil (about half full). Heat slowly to 375 degrees.
5. Add as many pieces of dough at a time as will float one layer deep. Fry until light brown, turning as necessary. Drain on absorbent paper.
6. Put honey and sugar into a small pan; place over low heat for about 5 minutes. Set aside but keep warm.
7. Refrigerate until slightly chilled. Arrange on serving plate. Sprinkle tiny candies over the top.

Crumb Cake

3 CUPS FLOUR
2 CUPS GRANULATED SUGAR
3 TEASPOONS BAKING POWDER
PINCH OF SALT
2 TEASPOONS VANILLA EXTRACT OR CINNAMON EXTRACT
3/4 CUP SOLID WHITE VEGETABLE SHORTENING
1 CUP MILK
2 EGGS
1/4 CUP MARGARINE

1. Preheat oven to 350 degrees.
2. In a large bowl, mix together flour, sugar, baking powder, salt, and vanilla extract. Add the shortening, and mix batter with a fork to form pea-sized pieces.
3. Place 1 cup of flour mixture in a small bowl and set it aside.
4. To the flour mixture in the larger bowl, add milk and eggs; mix with an electric beater on medium for 3 minutes.
5. To the small bowl mixture, add margarine; mix well with your fingers to form small or large crumbs.
6. Grease with shortening and flour a 9 × 13–inch baking pan.
7. Add the cake mixture to the pan, and top with the crumbs.
8. Bake in oven for 45 minutes.
9. Cake is done when a toothpick, inserted in center, comes out clean.
10. Makes about 20 servings.

Linzertorte Cookies

Serves 16

2 3/4 CUPS FLOUR
1 CUP MARGARINE, ROOM TEMPERATURE
1/2 CUP SUGAR
3 OUNCES CREAM CHEESE, ROOM TEMPERATURE
1 EGG, ROOM TEMPERATURE
1/2 TEASPOON VANILLA EXTRACT
GOOD PRESERVES, SUCH AS STRAWBERRY, CHERRY,
AMOUNT VARIES ON SIZE OF COOKIE

1. In a large bowl, cream margarine and sugar.
2. Add cream cheese and egg, blending and mixing everything.
3. Add flour and mix well.
4. Refrigerate several hours or overnight.
5. Roll out dough to about 1/4 inch thick.
6. Cut out small circles, using a small cookie cutter, whiskey glass, or coffee measuring cup.
7. In the center of half of the circles, cut out a smaller circle or a design of your choice. This half will be the tops of the cookies, and the other half will be the bottoms.
8. Bake at 350 degrees on a greased cookie sheet for a few minutes before completely baked. Take out the cookie sheet, and cover the bottom halves with the preserves; place the top of cookie over the jam, and place back in the oven for 1–2 minutes.
9. Take out of oven, and place the cookies onto a rack to allow them to cool.

Note: When a recipe tells you to cream butter and sugar, it means that you should beat the two ingredients with a wooden spoon and a bit of elbow grease until they form a light, uniform, and creamy mixture. Once sugar and butter are properly creamed, the sugar crystals will have dissolved, resulting in a smooth texture.[21]

No-Roll Tart or Pie Dough

1 1/4 CUPS FLOUR
DASH OF SALT
3 TABLESPOONS SUGAR
1/4 TEASPOON BAKING POWDER
6 TABLESPOONS BUTTER
1 LARGE EGG

1. In a medium mixing bowl, combine flour, salt, sugar, and baking powder.
2. Cut butter into 6–8 pieces, and distribute over dry ingredients.
3. Using finger tips or pastry blender, mix in the butter finely, until mixture resembles a fine powder. Be careful not to make it pasty.
4. Beat egg with a fork in a small bowl, and stir into mixture. It should remain dry and crumbly.
5. Turn dough into a buttered 10–11 inch tart pan with a removable bottom, or into a 9-inch pie pan.
6. Distribute evenly around bottom and side of pan; press into place with floured finger tips. Slide into plastic bag, and chill while preparing filling. See peach crumble pie recipe on page X.

Pastry Tarts

Serves 10

2 CUPS SIFTED FLOUR
1/2 TEASPOON SALT
2/3 CUP SHORTENING
4 TABLESPOONS WATER
MILK FOR BRUSHING

For Filling

1 CUP CUT-UP APRICOTS, DATES, OR RAISINS
(YOU MAY MIX FRUITS IF DESIRED)
1/2 CUP SUGAR
1/2 CUP WATER
NUTS (OPTIONAL AFTER COOKING)

1. Heat oven to 450 degrees for baking.
2. In a small skillet, cook the filling ingredients on medium heat until thick, about 5 minutes.
3. Mix flour and salt; cut in shortening. Sprinkle with water, and mix well with a fork.
4. Divide dough in half. Flatten each half slightly, and roll into a rectangle (8 by 12 inches).
5. Cut each half into 6 (4-inch) squares.
6. Put 1 tablespoon of filling in center of each square. Moisten edges of pastry with water, bring up corner to center, and seal.
7. Brush with milk, sprinkle with sugar, and bake on cookie sheet for 15–20 minutes.

Returning crusaders introduced pastry tarts to Europe. Italian Renaissance chefs are credited with perfecting these sweets. Greece and France also adopted these pastries into their cuisines.

Peach Crumble Pie

Serves 6-8

1 NO-ROLL PIE-DOUGH SHELL (SEE PAGE 108)
FOR TOPPING
1/2 CUP BUTTER
1/2 CUP LIGHT BROWN SUGAR, PACKED
1 1/4 CUPS FLOUR

For Peach Filling

2 1/2 POUNDS FRAGRANT, RIPE, FREESTONE PEACHES
1/4 CUP GRANULATED SUGAR
1 TABLESPOON FLOUR
1 TEASPOON FINELY GRATED LEMON ZEST

1. For the topping, melt the butter; stir in sugar and flour. Let stand for 5 minutes. Using fingertips, break into large crumbs.
2. For the filling, cut a shallow cross into the top of the peaches. Plunge them a few times into boiling water, about 30 seconds. Remove to a bowl of cold water, and slip off the skins. If the peaches are ripe, the skins will come off easily. If they do not come off easily, then use a paring knife.
3. Halve and pit the peaches, and then cut each half into 5–6 wedges. Place in a bowl, and sprinkle with sugar, flour, and lemon zest. Toss well to coat.
4. Spoon into no-roll pie shell; sprinkle crumb topping evenly over the filling.
5. Bake at 350 degrees on lowest rack in the oven for 30–40 minutes until the filling is bubbling and the crumbs are well colored.

Note: You may use apples, stewed apricots, or prunes as variations to the filling.

Peach crumble pie is also known as cobbler, tart, or torte, among various other names. Early settlers of America brought their favorite recipes with them. They had to use whatever was available to them, and that is how all the different names came about. Peach crumble pie was served as the main course for breakfast. It wasn't until the nineteenth century that it became mainly a dessert.[22]

Struffoli

Serves 8-10

1 3/4–2 CUPS FLOUR
1/4 TEASPOON SALT
3 EGGS
1/2 TEASPOON VANILLA EXTRACT
1 CUP HONEY
1 TABLESPOON SUGAR
VEGETABLE OIL, FOR DEEP FRYING
1 TABLESPOON TINY, MULTICOLORED CANDIES

1. Put 1 cup of flour and salt into a medium bowl; make a well in the center. Add 1 egg at a time, mixing slightly after each addition. Add vanilla extract. Stir in more of the flour to make a soft dough.
2. Turn dough onto a floured surface, and knead until dough is smooth and elastic. Cover and let stand to breathe, about 30 minutes.
3. Divide into halves or quarters. Lightly roll each section into a rectangle approximately 1/4 to 1/2 inch thick. Cut into 1/4- to 1/2-inch strips. Using the palm of your hands to roll to pencil thickness, cut into 1/4- to 1/2-inchi pieces and roll into little balls.
4. Fill a deep frying pan with vegetable oil about half full; heat slowly to 375 degrees.
5. Add as many pieces of dough at a time as will float one layer deep. Fry until light brown, turning as necessary. Drain on absorbent paper.
6. Put honey and sugar into a small pan; place over low heat about 5 minutes. Set aside but keep warm.
7. Refrigerate until slightly chilled. Arrange on serving plate. Sprinkle tiny candies over the top.

Zeppole

Serves 4-5

2 LARGE EGGS
1/2 POUND RICOTTA
1 TEASPOON VANILLA EXTRACT
1 CUP FLOUR
2 TEASPOONS BAKING POWDER
2 TEASPOONS SUGAR
OLIVE OIL OR VEGETABLE OIL, FOR FRYING
POWDERED SUGAR, FOR SPRINKLING

1. Beat eggs. Add vanilla extract and ricotta; mix well.
2. In a medium bowl, mix flour, sugar, and baking powder. Add egg mixture and mix. You may use an electric mixer at low speed.
3. Heat oil to about 375 degrees. Take about a tablespoon of flour mixture, and drop it into the hot vegetable oil. The zeppoles will usually turn over by themselves, but watch and turn them over if they do not. Cook for about 4 minutes.
4. When done, place the zeppoles on paper towels or thick napkins, where they will drain.
5. Sprinkle powdered sugar on the zeppoles.

References

(1)   Lasagna. https://en.wikipedia.org/wiki/Lasagne (1a) http://historia-de-victuals.blogspot.com/2011/07/july-is-lasagna-awareness-month.html

(2)   Artichoke. http://parkridgeeasthospital.com/hl/?/21516/Artichoke

(3)   Calzone. https://en.wikipedia.org/wiki/Calzone

(4)   Eggplant Parm. http://www.cliffordawright.com/caw/food/entries/display.php/topic_id/4/id/109/

(5)   Squash. http://www.newworldencyclopedia.org/entry/Squash_(plant)

(6)   Blanch. http://localfoods.about.com/od/preparationtips/qt/How-To-Blanch.htm

(7)   Gently Fold. http://www.incredibleegg.org/egg-facts/eggcyclopedia/c/cooking-terms

(8)   Pizza Rustica. http://www.schoolofflaunt.com/blogpost-61193/Pizza-RusticaItalian-Easter-Pie-By-Franco-Lania.html

(9)   Green Bean. http://www.cliffordawright.com/caw/food/entries/display.php/id/5/

(10)   Bruschetta. http://oilandvinegar.cruets.com/332/bruschetta-an-italian-bread-dis

(11)   Marinara Sauce. https://en.wikipedia.org/wiki/Tomato

(12)   Ragu. https://en.wikipedia.org/wiki/Rag%C3%B9

(13)   Braciole "Braciola." https://en.wikipedia.org/wiki/Braciola (accessed February 2, 2015).

(14)   Cacciatore. http://trevsbistro.com/2012/12/11/tuesdays-project-chicken-cacciatore-or-hunters-chicken/

(15)   Meatballs. https://suite.io/christopher-t-reilly/1h8h2cy

(16)   Meatloaf. http://www.care2.com/greenliving/5-things-you-didnt-know-about-the-history-of-meatloaf.html

17) Pot Roast. http://www.thriftyfoods.com/EN/main/cook/tips-tricks/cooking-tips/meat/history-pot-roast.htm

(18) Roast Chicken. https://en.wikipedia.org/wiki/List_of_chicken_breeds

(19) Paste e Fagioli. http://www.delallo.com/articles/zuppa-italian-comfort-food … … http://www.chelseagreen.com/blogs/what-is-the-poor-mans-meat/

(20) Springform Pan. https://en.wikipedia.org/wiki/Springform_pan

(21) Cream Butter and Sugar. http://www.cookthink.com/reference/1608/What_does_it_mean_to_cream_butter_and_sugar

(22) Peach Crumble Pie. http://whatscookingamerica.net/History/CobblerHistory.htm